SPIDERS

Tom Jackson

Grolier
an imprint of

www.scholastic.com/librarypublishing

Published 2008 by Grolier
An imprint of Scholastic Library Publishing
Old Sherman Turnpike, Danbury,
Connecticut 06816

For The Brown Reference Group plc
Project Editor: Jolyon Goddard
Copy-editors: Ann Baggaley, Lisa Hughes
Picture Researcher: Clare Newman
Designers: Jeni Child, Lynne Ross,
    Sarah Williams
Managing Editor: Bridget Giles

Volume ISBN-13: 978-0-7172-6287-8
Volume ISBN-10: 0-7172-6287-1

**Library of Congress
Cataloging-in-Publication Data**

Nature's children. Set 3.
    p. cm.
Includes bibliographical references and
index.
ISBN 13: 978-0-7172-8082-7
ISBN 10: 0-7172-8082-9
1. Animals--Encyclopedias, Juvenile. 1.
Grolier Educational (Firm)
QL49.N384 2008
590.3--dc22
                              2007031568

Printed and bound in China

PICTURE CREDITS

Front Cover: **Shutterstock**: Shachar Weis.

Back Cover: **Nature PL**: Kim Taylor;
Shutterstock: Anyka, Cathy Keifer.

Ardea: Densey Clyne/Ascape 29; **Corbis**:
David Rosebury 38; **FLPA**: Roger
Wilmshurst 14; **Nature PL**: Ingo Arndt 10,
Nick Garbutt 41, Duncan McEwan 18,
Pete Oxford 2–3, 34; **NHPA**: A. N. T. Photo
Library 21, James Carmichael Jr. 22, 46;
Shutterstock: David Ascota Allely 30, John
Bell 45, Cathy Keifer 4, 5, 9, 17, Hway Kiong
Lim 26–27, Ellie Mae 13, Christopher Meder
33, Scott T. Slattery 6, Chelmodeev
Alexander Vasilyerick 42, Judy Worley 37.

Contents

Fact File: Spiders 4

Spying Spiders 7

Body Double 8

Masters Spinners 11

Weaving a Web 12

King Weaver 15

Sticky Situation 16

Trip Wires 19

Springing the Trap 20

Flesh Soup 23

All Eyes 24

Jump to It 25

Feature Photo 26–27

Sprint and Swing 28

Invisible Hunters 31

Mating Dance 32

Basket of Eggs 35

Huge Families 36

Taking to the Air 39

Too Big for Its Skin 40

Hunted Hunters 43

Hairy Monster? 44

Dangerous Duo 47

Friendly and Helpful 48

Words to Know 49

Find Out More 51

Index 52

FACT FILE: Spiders

Class	Arachnids (Arachnida)
Order	Spiders (Araneae)
Families	More than 100 families worldwide; 23 families of spiders in North America
Genera	Hundreds of genera worldwide; 116 genera of spiders in North America
Species	There are about 40,000 species worldwide; at least 3,000 species of spiders in North America
World distribution	All parts of the world except the oceans, Antarctica, and other ice-capped regions
Habitat	Almost all habitats except sea water
Distinctive physical characteristics	Eight legs, body made of two parts, spinnerets on abdomen (rear section) produce silk
Habits	Many species build a web out of silk for trapping prey; silk is also used to wrap eggs
Diet	Insects, worms, small birds, reptiles, and mammals

Introduction

Spiders are eight-legged creatures that range greatly in size. The smallest spiders are the size of a pinhead and the largest ones can cover a dinner plate when their legs are extended. Spiders are accomplished hunters. They produce silk, and many use the silk to make sticky webs that trap **prey**. Spiders have fangs that inject **venom** into their prey to stop it from moving. Few spiders can harm humans. In fact, most spiders actually help humans by eating insect pests.

A female wolf spider climbs over a rock.

A black and yellow
garden spider sits
in her web. This
spider prefers to
live in a sunny site
among flowers
and tall plants.

Spying Spiders

Spiders live in houses and backyards. They also live in deserts, fields, forests, on mountaintops, and in swamps. There are even spiders that dive underwater. In fact, spiders can be found all over the world, with the exception of Antarctica and other ice-capped regions.

Biologists, or scientists who study animals and plants, have identified about 40,000 species, or types, of spiders in the world. At least 3,000 of those live in North America. In fact, there are probably many more species of spiders, but biologists have not had enough time to discover them yet.

Body Double

Spiders are often confused with insects. In fact, spiders are a completely different kind of animal. If you compare spiders and insects up close you can see the differences. An insect's body, such as that of a wasp, butterfly, or beetle, has three sections. Insects also have six legs, and many of them have wings.

Spiders never have wings. They have eight legs, and a body made of just two sections. The rear body section is called the abdomen. The front part is the cephalothorax (SEFFA-LA-THOR-AKS). All the legs grow out of this front section. Spiders also have two armlike feelers, or **palpi**, at the front of the cephalothorax.

Spiders do have some relatives, which share this body structure. Together with spiders, these creatures are called the **arachnids**. Other arachnids include scorpions, harvestmen, and mites.

Like all spiders, this wolf spider's legs grow out of its cephalothorax—the front section of its body.

The weight of this orb-web spider is supported by a single silk thread.

Master Spinners

Spiders are not the only animals that make silk. The material used to make silk clothes is actually made by caterpillars. Most spiders spend their whole lives making silk and are expert spinners. Spiders' silk is extremely strong. It is true that humans can tear up a cobweb very easily, but that is because the silken strands in it are very, very thin. If you compare a thread of spiders' silk to a steel wire of the same thickness, the silk is much stronger.

Spiders produce silk using special **glands** on their abdomen called **spinnerets**. Liquid silk is squeezed through tiny holes at the tips of the spinnerets. The liquid dries into a very fine thread of silk. Spiders can spin threads of any length. The silk just keeps on coming through the spinnerets, and the thread grows longer and longer. Spiders make different types of silk. They use dry silk for ropes and building shelters. Sticky silk is used in webs.

Weaving a Web

Spiders use silk in many ways. They wrap their eggs in silken bags. They spin silk safety ropes when climbing in trees. Wherever a spider goes, it leaves behind a silken **drag-line**. That serves as a lifeline that leads the spider back to where it came from, especially if it is in danger.

Most spiders use silk to make a web. A spider's web acts like a net for trapping insects and other prey. Spiders build many different web shapes. The funnel-web spiders of Australia, as their name suggests, make their webs in a funnel shape. Some spiders build webs close to the ground to catch crawling insects. But most spiders create large, spiral webs that hang in the air to catch flying insects. The threads of silk are so thin that the webs are almost invisible. Buzzing flies and other unwary prey usually don't even see the web and fly straight into it.

In fall spiderwebs are everywhere. Female spiders are hungriest at this time of year and they build as many webs as they can.

This garden spider is anchored to its web by a silk safety line. If the spider falls it can use the line to guide itself back to the web.

An orb-web spider weaves the spiral sections of its web. The web will last about a day before it needs repairing.

King Weaver

Some of the most skilled web builders are the orb-web spiders. These common garden spiders come in a variety of shapes and colors.

To build its web, the spider needs two upright supports, such as branches or stalks, to hang the web from. First, the spider releases a thread from the top of one support. The thread is then carried by the breeze across to the second upright, making a bridge. Next, the spider hangs a Y-shape of threads from this bridge. The Y-shape has more threads added to make spokes, before a spiral of threads is added on top. The entire construction of the web is completed by the spider in less than an hour!

Sticky Situation

Once an insect flies into a web, it has little chance of escaping. The spokes of the web and the central section are made with dry thread. Orb-webs and many other spiders wait motionless at the center of their web holding on to the dry thread. Most of the spiral section is made of sticky threads. These threads are what trap the spider's victims. They are covered in a gummy liquid that glues the insects to the web. The more the victims struggle, the more tangled they become. The spider waiting at the center of the web can feel where the struggling prey is by the vibrations running through the web. It makes its way over to its victim, being sure to walk on only the dry threads. It is very rare for a spider to become fatally trapped in its own web. When the spider reaches its prey, it kills the insect by injecting it with a paralysing venom.

A jumping spider sinks its fangs into a fly.

A funnel-web spider sits in its web waiting for prey. This type of spider prefers to make its lair in a damp, sheltered area.

Trip Wires

Not all web-weaving spiders sit at the center of their webs. Many larger species would be too easy to spot out in the open. These spiders stay hidden out of sight in a nearby lair. They stay in touch with what is happening in their web via a silk thread. This thread runs from their lair to their web. The spider always has one foot on the thread to make sure it does not miss anything. When a victim crashes into the web, the shockwaves make the communication line move. The spider then knows that it has caught something in its web. One group of spiders that does that is the funnel-web spiders. These spiders live at the bottom of a tube of silk that opens out into a wide sheet of tangled silk.

Webs are very effective traps, but they get damaged easily. Most spiders have to spin a new one every night, although some just have to make repairs—patching up any holes with more sticky threads.

Springing the Trap

Some spiders do not catch prey in a web. Instead, they build other ingenious traps. The trap-door spider lives in a hole in the ground. It digs this den by shoveling earth with its fangs. It then carefully plasters the walls with sand mixed with saliva. That makes the hole waterproof. Next the spider lines its home with some soft silk to make it more cozy. Lastly, it weaves itself a door that fits exactly over the entrance and even has a silken hinge to keep it in place.

With the trap-door shut, the spider is warm and dry inside its lair. It does not have to leave home to get food. The spider has sensitive hairs on its legs that pick up the vibrations of insects strolling around on the ground above. When an insect comes close to the nest, the spider bursts through the trap-door and snatches its victim.

Most trap-door spiders dig a single tunnel in the ground. But some of these spiders make side tunnels leading from the main lair.

A bird-dropping spider sucks up fly soup.

Flesh Soup

Spiders kill their victims by biting them with their two fangs. The fangs are not teeth, like a tiger or a snake has, however, but rather mouthparts with sharp tips. Venom is pumped through the fangs into the prey's body. This poison paralyses the victim.

Most animals digest their food after they swallow it. The food mixes with chemicals in their stomach. The chemicals break down the solid lumps of food into a broth of nutrients. Their body takes these nutrients and uses them to run itself. Spiders have a very narrow mouth and cannot chew their food. They actually digest their food before they swallow it. They do this by squirting chemicals into their victim's body. The chemicals turn the insides of their prey into a meaty soup. The spider then sucks up this soup through its small, tube-shaped mouth.

If the spider has caught several insects in its web, it might not eat all of them immediately. It wraps the leftovers in silk and hangs them from its web for later, when it is hungry again.

All Eyes

Spiders have a lot of eyes. Two are just not enough for most spiders and some have as many as eight. A spider's eyes are on its cephalothorax. The largest ones point forward. But some are positioned to look up and to the sides as well.

An animal with so many eyes should be able to see very well. But, in fact, most spiders are nearsighted. Their tube-shaped eyes work differently from human eyes. They can detect movement well. But they are not very good at seeing details.

Some spiders, however, have excellent vision. Jumping spiders have eight very large eyes, which take up more room than their brain. Jumping spiders can spot prey that is 8 feet (2.4 m) away. A jumping spider is less than half an inch (1.25 cm) long, so that is a long way for it to be able to see. It would be like a human being able to see a face from 1,200 feet (360 m) away!

Jump to It

Spiders are very acrobatic creatures. Jumping spiders may be the most acrobatic of all the spiders. As well as having excellent vision, jumping spiders can also leap huge distances. These spiders can travel 40 times their own body length in one jump! That is like an adult man jumping three-quarters of the length of a football field.

Jumping spiders do not spin webs. They stalk their prey silently, using their large eyes to keep track of where a victim is. Once the spider is in pouncing distance, it ties itself to a branch with an anchor line and leaps onto its victim. The jumping spider's good vision allows it to judge how far it needs to jump very accurately, and it rarely misses its prey. Once it has caught a meal, the spider climbs up the anchor line to feed sitting on its perch.

All the eyes of this jumping spider are on the lookout for prey.

Sprint and Swing

The jumping spider is not the only spider that hunts without spinning a web. The wolf is an expert hunter that uses stealth and speed to catch its prey. The wolf spider does the same thing. This spider hunts on the ground for beetles and grasshoppers. It sits motionless as it scans the area for prey. Once it sees one, the spider dashes after it. The wolf spider has very long legs, making it one of the fastest sprinters in the spider world. Few insects can outrun a wolf spider.

Perhaps the most unusual spider hunter is the bolas spider. This species "fishes" for moths. At night the spider sits on a high branch, swinging a long thread back and forth. The thread has a blob of sticky silk at the end, which is coated with chemicals that make it smell like a moth. This smell attracts real moths to the blob, which then get stuck to the spider's silk. Dinner is served!

A bolas spider has
"reeled in" a moth.

A crab spider will
wait motionless on
a flower until its
prey appears.

Invisible Hunters

Spiders are colored in certain ways so that they blend in with their surroundings. This is called **camouflage**. Some spiders are very good at remaining unseen, including the bird dropping spider, which sits on tree trunks and leaves. Its black and white markings make it look like, well, bird droppings. Another spider pretends to be an ant by walking on just six legs instead of eight. The ants unknowingly allow this predator into their nest, and then the spider feasts on its unsuspecting prey.

Crab spiders are the best camouflage artists of the spider world. These little spiders hunt for insects on brightly colored flowers. A crab spider lurks on petals and can change its colors to match those of the flowers. When an insect lands on the flower in search of nectar, the crab spider is ready to attack.

Mating Dance

It is not easy being a male spider. In many species, the male spider is much smaller than the female. Sometimes, the female is 20 times bigger, which leaves the male looking like a completely different type of spider. A male spider needs to be brave to attract a **mate**. If the female he approaches is not interested, he might end up as her next meal!

A male has a special way of letting a female know he wants to mate. He crawls to the edge of her web and taps out a message on one of the threads. Each species of spider uses a unique code or rhythm to send its message. If the female is interested, she taps back a greeting, and the male crawls closer. Some males then dance for their mate, while others try to win her over with a gift of food. If all goes well, the female lets the male mate with her. But he does not hang around afterwards—she might decide to eat him after all!

A female golden orb spider sits on a web with a much smaller male.

The egg sacs of a black widow spider hang on its web.

Basket of Eggs

Spiders' eggs do not have a hard protective shell, like the eggs of a bird or turtle. Instead, the gel-like spiders' eggs are kept safe in a soft basket woven from their mother's silk. Biologists call these baskets "egg sacs." Most species of spiders hide the egg sacs away in a dark corner to allow the eggs to develop safely. Often the egg sacs are camouflaged with twigs and leaves.

Sometimes, female spiders hang their egg sac in their web, so they can watch over it day and night. Other spiders prefer to carry their egg sacs with them at all times, attached to the underside of their abdomen. Sometimes the egg sac is so large that the female spider has to walk on the tips of its legs to keep the sac off the ground!

Huge Families

By keeping their egg sacs safe, female spiders can be sure that most of the eggs will hatch into baby spiders, or **spiderlings**. Some egg sacs produce many thousands of spiderlings. Most of the young spiders do not survive for long. They are easy prey for insects, birds, small animals, and even other spiders.

Spiderlings look like miniature adult spiders, except for the fact that their skin is so thin it is almost see-through. Most spiderlings leave their mother immediately, and start to weave tiny webs of their own. But some types of spiderlings stay close to their mother for longer. For example, the nursery-web spider builds a special tent for her spiderlings to live in. And baby wolf spiders travel on their mother's back until they are too heavy for her to carry them. It is then time for them to hunt alone.

A mother wolf spider will go on hunting as usual while carrying her young on her back.

Newly hatched garden spiders disperse.

Taking to the Air

When spiderlings are ready to leave home, the quickest way for them to travel is by air. Spiderlings cannot fly like birds or insects. But they are small enough to be blown by the wind. This method of travel is known as **ballooning**. To begin ballooning a spider climbs to the top of a tree, where the wind is stronger. It then spins several strands of very thin silk called **gossamer**. That acts as a sail or kite to catch the breeze.

Once airborne, spiders can travel for miles. Ballooning spiderlings have been known to cross hundreds of miles of sea. Some spiderlings reach heights of 14,000 feet (4,200 meters). We know that because they sometimes get squashed against the windshield of planes that are flying very high! If the spiderlings don't like where they land, they can take another flight.

Too Big for Its Skin

A spider does not have bones inside its body. Instead, its skeleton—the hard parts that give the body its shape—is on the outside. This hard shell acts like a suit of armor. It is called an **exoskeleton**. Unfortunately, a spider's exoskeleton does not stretch very well. Unlike skin, an exoskeleton does not grow as the spider gets older. Eventually a spider's exoskeleton becomes so tight that it bursts. Fortunately, the spider has a new one ready underneath. When the old skeleton finally breaks open completely, the spider steps out of it. The new skeleton is a little soft at first. The spider pumps air into it to make it as large as possible. The outer covering then hardens up, but now there is plenty of room inside for the spider to grow.

While shedding its old exoskeleton, a giant huntsman spider from Borneo is vulnerable to attack from predators.

A praying mantis has powerful jaws that can easily chomp through a garden spider.

Hunted Hunters

Spiders are expert killers, but that doesn't mean they are not attacked themselves. Birds, frogs, rats, and even fish will eat them if they get the chance. Some spiders are even preyed on by other spiders. One species of jumping spider has an especially devious way of doing this. It taps a love message into its prey's web. When the victim comes to welcome its new mate, the jumping spider pounces.

Insects also prey on spiders. A praying mantis snatches spiders from their webs using its long swordlike arms. Some wasps sting spiders— which temporarily stops the spider from moving—and lay their eggs on the spider's body. When these eggs hatch, the maggotlike young pierce the exoskeleton of the spider and eat it alive from the inside out!

Hairy Monster?

Tarantulas are very hairy and fierce-looking spiders. They are also the largest spiders in the world. In North America, tarantulas reach about 3 inches (8 cm) long. They are three times that wide measuring from legs to legs. The world's largest spider is a tarantula living in South America. Called the Goliath bird-eating spider, it is as big as a dinner plate.

Despite their size, tarantulas are pretty harmless to people. They do bite, but their bite is only as painful as a bee sting. They also release stinging hairs from their legs, which can irritate the skin, but are not dangerous.

Despite its name, the Goliath bird-eating spider prefers insects and small lizards and frogs to birds.

Silk is released from the spinnerets of a female black widow spider.

Dangerous Duo

Some spiders are deadly. Australia has many dangerous species, including the Sydney funnel-web, which has very poisonous venom. People have died from funnel-web bites, but for the most part these spiders are shy and rarely bite. The most dangerous spider in the world is the Brazilian wandering spider. Its venom is very strong. But unlike the Sydney funnel-web, this spider is very aggressive, and each year it bites several people.

There are only two dangerous spiders in North America: the black widow and the brown recluse. The brown recluse is also known as the fiddleback, because it has the shape of a violin on its back. It lives in the southern United States. A bite from a recluse spider will never kill a human, but it will hurt for a very long time.

Black widows, however, are deadly. Only the female bites. Fortunately most people survive after a visit to the hospital. Black widows are easy to spot. They have a red hourglass shape on their black belly.

Friendly and Helpful

In the past doctors used spiders and their webs to make medicines. Although most doctors wouldn't prescribe a spider as a cure today, spiders' silk does contain chemicals that can kill germs. Some people have even managed to use spiders' silk to make clothes!

Spiders are very important. Each of these little hunters kills hundreds of insects a year. Together that adds up to many billions of insects. That includes insects that damage garden plants and crops. If spiders didn't kill them, there would be billions more insects flying and crawling around.

Words to Know

Arachnids Members of the class Arachnida, including spiders, scorpions, ticks, and mites.

Ballooning A method of travel used by young spiders. They float through the air hanging from silken threads that are carried by the wind.

Camouflage Markings or coloring that help an animal blend into the background.

Drag-line A silken line made and used by spiders to secure them to one spot. When in danger, a spider climbs back up its drag-line.

Exoskeleton The hard outer covering of a spider's body.

Glands The parts of a spider's body that produce silk.

Gossamer	Threads small spiders spin in order to balloon.
Mate	Either member of a breeding pair; to come together to produce young.
Palpi	The name given to a spider's feelers.
Prey	Animals hunted by other animals for food.
Spiderlings	Baby spiders.
Spinnerets	The parts of their body that spiders use to spin their webs and lines.
Venom	A poisonous fluid.

Find Out More

Books

Allman, T. *From Spider Webs to Man-made Silk.* Detroit, Michigan: KidHaven Press, 2005.

Murawski, D. *Spiders and their Webs.* Washington, D.C.: National Geographic, 2004.

Web sites

Spiders
www.enchantedlearning.com/themes/spiders.shtml
Rhymes, pictures to print and color in, and craft ideas.

Tarantulas
www.desertmuseum.org/kids/features_tarantulas.html
Facts about tarantulas in the Arizona desert.

Index

A, B, C

abdomen 8, 11, 35
anchor line 25
arachnids 8
ballooning 39
bird dropping spider
       22, 31
bite 23, 44, 47
black widow spider 34,
       46, 47
bolas spider 28, 29
Brazilian wandering
       spider 47
brown recluse spider 47
camouflage 31, 35
cephalothorax 8, 9, 24
climbing 12, 25
communication 19, 32
crab spider 30, 31

D, E, F

digestion 23
drag-line 12
egg sac 34, 35, 36
eggs 12
exoskeleton 40, 41, 43
eyes 24, 27

eyesight 24, 25, 28
fangs 5, 17, 20, 23
food 12, 17, 22, 23, 25,
       28, 32
funnel-web spider 12, 18,
       19, 47

G, H, I

garden spider 6, 13, 38,
       42
giant huntsman spider
       41
golden orb spider 33
Goliath bird-eating spider
       44, 45
gossamer 39
habitat 7
hunting 5, 28, 31, 36, 37
insects 5, 8, 12, 16, 20, 23,
       28, 31, 39, 43, 48

J, L, M

jumping spiders 17, 24,
       25, 27, 43
lair 19, 20
legs 5, 8, 20, 21, 28, 35, 44
mating 32

N, O, P

nursery-web spider 36
orb-web spider 10, 14,
       15, 16
palpi 8
praying mantis 42, 43
predator 41, 43
prey 5, 12, 16, 18, 19, 20,
       23, 25, 28, 30, 31

R, S, T

relatives 8
silk 5, 10, 11, 12, 13, 19,
       20, 23, 28, 35, 39,
       46, 48
spiderlings 35, 37,
       38, 39
spinnerets 11, 46
tarantulas 44
trap-door spider 20, 21

V, W

venom 16, 23, 47
web 5, 6, 11, 12, 13, 14, 15,
       16, 18, 19, 20, 23, 32,
       33, 34, 35, 36, 43, 48
wolf spider 5, 9, 28, 36, 37